SMARTASS AFFIRMATIONS

SMARTASS AFFIRMATIONS

WISDOM FROM THE WATER HOSE GENERATION

SMART AZZ AUNTIE

RHONDA JAMES

MIAMI

Published by Mango Publishing, a division of Mango Publishing Group, Inc.

Cover Design: Elina Diaz
Cover Photo/Illustration: ysbrandcosijn/stock.adobe.com
Layout & Design: Elina Diaz
Author Photo: Roselyn Photography

For permission requests, please contact the publisher at:
Mango Publishing Group
5966 South Dixie Highway, Suite 300
Miami, FL 33143
info@mango.bz

For special orders, quantity sales, course adoptions and corporate sales, please email the publisher at sales@mango.bz. For trade and wholesale sales, please contact Ingram Publisher Services at customer.service@ingramcontent.com or +1.800.509.4887.

Smartass Affirmations: Wisdom from the Water Hose Generation

Library of Congress Cataloging-in-Publication number: requested
ISBN: (print) 978-1-68481-894-5, (ebook) 978-1-68481-895-2
BISAC category code: SEL004000 SELF-HELP / Affirmations

TABLE OF CONTENTS

MY SON

INTRODUCTION

If you grew up drinking from the water hose, riding your bike until the streetlights came on, and making mixtapes from the radio with your finger on the "record" button, congratulations; you survived childhood without a helmet, a smartphone, or a helicopter parent. And somehow, you still turned out pretty damn amazing.

This book is for *us* ♥: the latchkey kids, the cereal-for-dinner survivors, the masters of "figuring it out" long before Google existed. We are the generation that knew freedom before Wi-Fi, fun before filters, and consequences before participation trophies. We are the bridge between analog and digital, the keepers of phone numbers in our heads, and the last ones to truly understand the pain of losing a cassette in the tape deck.

These affirmations aren't the soft, whispery kind you tape to your mirror and repeat in your yoga voice. Nope. These are water hose affirmations: equal parts grit, humor, nostalgia, and straight talk. They're here to remind you of who you are, where you came from, and why you're still here kicking ass (even if your knees sound like bubble wrap).

So grab your Capri-Sun, adjust your Walkman, and settle in. This is your permission slip to laugh, reminisce, and own your badassery—water hose vibes and all.

CASSETTE

ACKNOWLEDGMENTS

First off, let me give a warm, nostalgic shoutout to my fellow water hose generation readers, you glorious, sarcastic, semi-traumatized survivors of latchkey living, rotary phones, and unfiltered tap water. This book is for you. And let's be real, if you didn't almost choke on a Now & Later or survive a car ride without a seatbelt, you're reading this on borrowed vibes.

To my parents: Thanks for raising me with the kind of love that said "Figure it out" and "Don't touch my thermostat" in the same breath. Your tough love made me resilient and deeply suspicious of authority. Mission accomplished.

To every teacher who put "Talks too much" on my report card, I turned it into a book, boo. Look at me now, running my mouth *with a purpose* and a font.

And back to the water hose generation, the generation that walked so the internet could run: We didn't get trophies for showing up, but we sure as hell earned every scar, every laugh line, and every ounce of wisdom in these pages.

We're not bitter; we're just seasoned.

AGING

I AM NOT TOO OLD, I'M JUST SEASONED LIKE A CAST-IRON SKILLET: TOUGH, LOYAL, AND FULL OF FLAVOR.

My grandma had one that was older than anyone in the family, and no matter what you cooked in it, that pan brought out the best flavor every single time. It was tough, reliable, and only got better with every meal.

That skillet taught me a lesson: aging doesn't mean losing your edge. It means building strength, loyalty, and character that you can't fake. Just like that pan, I've been through the heat. I've had my moments to sizzle, and now I bring something rich and full-flavored to the table, whether folks are ready for it or not.

I BELIEVE IN MYSELF, EVEN IF MY KNEES, BACK, AND PATIENCE GAVE UP IN 2013.

I LOVE AND ACCEPT MYSELF, EVEN WHEN I FORGET WHY I WALKED INTO A ROOM.

I MAY NOT KNOW WHERE MY READING GLASSES ARE, BUT I CAN STILL SPOT BS FROM ACROSS A ROOM.

I CHERISH MY ROOTS....EVEN THE GRAYS, BECAUSE EACH ONE REPRESENTS A PERSON I DIDN'T CUSS OUT.

I AM GROUNDED, UNLESS I BEND DOWN TOO FAST— THEN I'M DIZZY.

I AM NOT AGING; I AM MARINATING IN WISDOM, SARCASM, AND WINE.

I WALK WITH PURPOSE, PETTINESS, AND ORTHOPEDIC INSERTS.

In the '80s, we might've strutted down the block in Chuck Taylors, but now? These days, it's all about comfort meeting attitude.

I've earned every step: the ones that had me running from the laser tag guns, chasing the ice cream truck, or hustling to beat the school bell. And sure, now my feet might need a little extra support, but don't mistake that for slowing down.

Because beneath those orthopedic inserts is the same spirit that refused to back down from a dare, threw shade before "shade" was even a thing, and knew exactly when to throw a little petty side-eye to keep the peace.

I walk like I mean it: with purpose, a little attitude, and a whole lot of nostalgia packed into every step.

I AM NOT CRAZY; I AM HORMONALLY GIFTED.

I MAY HAVE BACK PAIN, BUT I ALSO HAVE WISDOM, WIT, AND A 380 IN MY PURSE.

I WILL REMIND MYSELF THAT AGING ISN'T A BURDEN, JUST A FULL-TIME IMPROV SHOW WITH NO SCRIPT.

I STRETCH DAILY.... MOSTLY ABOUT THE TRUTH AND HOW MUCH BACK PAIN I HAVE.

I STAY GROUNDED... BECAUSE GETTING UP TAKES PLANNING NOW.

I HONOR THE HEART OF MY YOUNGER SELF—THE ONE WHO BELIEVED ANYTHING WAS POSSIBLE.

I KNOW THAT EVEN IN TODAY'S WORLD, I CAN STILL CREATE THE MAGIC I GREW UP WITH.

NOSTALGIA

I SURVIVED DIAL-UP INTERNET, UNSUPERVISED SUMMERS, AND KOOL-AID WITH NO SUGAR. I FEAR NOTHING.

Back then, "getting online" meant announcing to the whole house that you were about to block the phone line for forty-five minutes. You'd click "connect" and listen to that screechy robot noise, praying nobody picked up the phone and ruined your chances of chatting on AOL.

Summers were a free-for-all. You left the house after breakfast and came back when the streetlights came on, sweaty and holding some random item you "borrowed" from a friend's garage. Lunch was usually a packet of Kool-Aid mixed with tap water and a hopeful stir, even though the sugar canister was mysteriously empty.

You could survive boredom without a screen, trust your gut on which friend's house had snacks, and still make it home in one piece without GPS. You learned early that life could throw anything at you and you'd handle it just fine. Which is why now, when chaos shows up, I don't flinch. I've been training for this my whole life.

I STILL REMEMBER PHONE NUMBERS, AND THAT'S MY SUPERPOWER.

I WATCHED SATURDAY MORNING CARTOONS, AND NOW I WATCH MY MOUTH. SOMETIMES.

I AM RESILIENT, SEASONED, AND STILL KNOW HOW TO MAKE A MIXTAPE FROM THE RADIO.

I AM NOT BEHIND; I'M JUST BUFFERING LIKE IT'S 1997.

I FORGIVE MYSELF FOR PAST MISTAKES—EXCEPT FOR THE MULLET PHASE.

I AM GROUNDED IN CASSETTE LOGIC AND WALKMAN WISDOM.

I REMEMBER WHEN PRIVACY WAS A DOOR, NOT A PASSWORD.

I HAVE PATIENCE, THANKS TO WAITING FOR AOL TO CONNECT.

I CAN HANDLE CHAOS. I SURVIVED NEW COKE.

I REMEMBER WHEN OUTSIDE WAS THE PLAN, NOT A PUNISHMENT.

Remember when the sun was your clock, and the world beyond your front door was a place full of endless possibilities? We didn't need screens to keep us entertained: just scraped knees, grass-stained clothes, and the sound of laughter echoing down the block.

Our days were spent chasing fireflies, building forts out of whatever we could find, and riding bikes until our legs ached. There was something pure about that kind of freedom, a kind of belonging that didn't require Wi-Fi or likes.

I think about those days often, and how they shaped the people we've become: the patience, the creativity, and the fierce independence that come from knowing the world is yours to explore. Outside was never a punishment; it was a gift. And I hope we never forget how to find that joy again.

I AM WHAT HAPPENS WHEN YOU RAISE KIDS WITHOUT BIKE HELMETS.

I AM NOT PRESSED; I LIVED THROUGH SHOULDER PADS.

I HONOR WHERE I'VE BEEN, EVEN IF IT WAS A MYSPACE PAGE.

I GREW UP ANALOG, BUT I GLOW UP DIGITAL.

I SMOKED CANDY CIGARETTES AND DRANK FROM THE WATER HOSE. I AM TO BE RESPECTED.

MY SPIRIT ANIMAL IS A BLOCKBUSTER MEMBERSHIP CARD.

I AM ROOTED IN THE STRENGTH OF A TIME WHEN NEIGHBORS KNEW YOUR NAME AND YOUR MAMA'S PHONE NUMBER.

I HONOR THE PATIENCE I LEARNED FROM WAITING FOR MIXTAPES TO RECORD ON CASSETTE.

VIDEO
CASSETTE

ZONTA
VIDEO CASSETTE
120
ULTRA COLOR
SUPER 120
HIGH GRADE TAPE
ULTRA HIGH QUALITY
VHS
NTSC Recording Time
SP 124 min.
LP 247 min.
EP 371 min.
STUDIO PERFORMANCE
MADE IN JAPAN
246 m

RESILIENCE

I DON'T BREAK; I PAUSE, REWIND, AND COME BACK WITH RECEIPTS.

Remember when we had to rewind VHS tapes before returning them to Blockbuster? There was no fast-forward button to skip the boring parts, no pause to catch your breath, just that clunky rewind that made that satisfying whirring noise. If you didn't rewind all the way, you got charged a fee, and nobody wanted that.

Life's kinda like that. When things get messy or overwhelming, I don't just snap. I take a moment: hitting rewind in my mind, going back over what happened, remembering every little detail, who said what, when, and how it all played out. I hold onto those memories like my own personal receipts, so when the time is right, I can show up with the full story.

Because breaking? That was what happened when you let the tape get all tangled up or chewed by the VCR. But me? I'm seasoned. I'm the one who learned how to handle the mess without losing my cool, rewinding carefully and coming back stronger, ready to set the record straight with a little side-eye and a lot of truth.

I MAKE PEACE WITH MY PAST....BUT DON'T TEST ME. I STILL REMEMBER YOUR MAMA'S PHONE NUMBER.

I RELEASE WHAT NO LONGER SERVES ME, LIKE LOW-RISE JEANS AND TOXIC PEOPLE.

I'M NOT STUCK; I'M STAYING STILL ON PURPOSE.

I'M ALLOWED TO OUTGROW PEOPLE, PANTS, AND PATIENCE.

I CAN FIX IT, DUCT TAPE IT, OR FORGET IT.

Growing up, duct tape was basically a magic wand. Broken chair leg? Duct tape. Hole in your jeans? Duct tape. That weird rattle in the car? Slap some duct tape on it and hope for the best.

We didn't have YouTube tutorials or quick online orders; we had to get creative and get it done with whatever was on hand. Sometimes that meant MacGyver-level fixes with bubble gum, safety pins, and yes, a whole lot of duct tape.

And if all else failed? Well, we just forgot about it and moved on, because survival was more important than perfection.

That's the spirit I carry with me: the patience to fix what I can, the courage to hold things together, and the grace to know when it's time to let go. That's water hose generation: tough, resourceful, and quietly unstoppable.

I AM ENOUGH, DESPITE WHAT THAT LITTLE VOICE SAYS DURING SWIMSUIT SEASON.

I TRUST THE TIMING IN MY LIFE, BUT I SIDE-EYE THE CALENDAR JUST IN CASE.

I CAN FORGIVE MISTAKES, BUT I WILL SCREENSHOT THEM FIRST.

I AM HEALED, AND I HAVE GROWN. BUT I STILL REMEMBER WHO DIDN'T RSVP TO MY PARTY IN 1998.

I AM GROUNDED IN THE RESILIENCE OF A GENERATION THAT MADE THEIR OWN FUN.

I AM GRATEFUL FOR THE GRIT THAT CAME FROM SOLVING PROBLEMS WITHOUT GOOGLE.

I ENDURED AOL CHAT ROOMS, SO I CAN SPOT RED FLAGS BEFORE THEY EVEN LOG ON.

I REWOUND VHS TAPES RELIGIOUSLY, WHICH TAUGHT ME THE POWER OF STARTING OVER.

I GREW UP WITH ONLY FOUR TV CHANNELS. PATIENCE AND CREATIVITY ARE HARDWIRED IN ME.

I RADIATE CONFIDENCE. MY SEATBELT WAS MOM'S ARM, AND LOOK AT ME NOW. UNSHAKEN.

CONVERSE
ALL STAR

ATTITUDE & SASS

I ACCEPT MYSELF FULLY, ESPECIALLY THE VERSION THAT SILENTLY JUDGES EVERYONE AT THE STORE.

Back in the day, we didn't have smartphones to distract us, so we paid attention—sometimes a little too much—to the people around us. When the grocery line moved slower than a dial-up connection, you'd watch that one person debate between Raisin Bran and Frosted Flakes like it was the ultimate life decision.

We learned to be patient in those moments, but also to notice the little things: the kid throwing a tantrum, the shopper who forgot their wallet, the cashier who was clearly done with everyone's nonsense. That quiet judgment was just part of how we processed the world before memes and emojis did it for us.

I accept that side of me now, because it's wrapped up in years of experience and a lifetime of watching people figure things out—sometimes with grace, sometimes with a lot of attitude. And honestly, that silent side-eye has saved me from a few headaches over the years.

I GIVE MYSELF GRACE, AND SIDE-EYE EVERYONE ELSE EQUALLY.

I AM A MAGNET FOR GOOD VIBES, SARCASM, AND UNNECESSARY GROUP TEXTS.

I DON'T CHASE, I ATTRACT.... ESPECIALLY BOXED WINE AND CLEARANCE RACKS.

I KEEP RECEIPTS IN MY DRAWER, IN MY PHONE, AND IN MY PETTY SPIRIT.

I'LL SUPPORT YOU, CLAP FOR YOU, AND STILL ROLL MY EYES IF YOU'RE BEING RIDICULOUS.

I'VE GOT OPINIONS, PLAYLISTS, AND KNEES THAT POP LIKE BUBBLE WRAP.

I'M A WALKING "I TOLD YOU SO."

I'M THE REASON PEOPLE SAY, "DON'T START NOTHING, WON'T BE NOTHING."

I DON'T SWEAT THE SMALL STUFF; I STIR THE BIG STUFF.

I'M THE ENERGY YOUR PARENTS WARNED YOU ABOUT, AND THEN SECRETLY LOVED.

I'M THE REASON THEY MADE "DON'T TRY THIS AT HOME" WARNINGS.

Growing up, rules were more like suggestions, and supervision was often a maybe. If there was a way to climb the tallest tree, jump off the highest swing, or rig up a skateboard with duct tape and hope for the best, you'd better believe I was the first in line.

I remember trying to build a zipline between two trees in the backyard using whatever rope and pulleys I could find. It didn't end well. There were scrapes, bruises, and more than one near-miss that had my parents shaking their heads—but secretly impressed.

We learned by doing, by failing spectacularly, and by figuring it out on our own, sometimes with a little reckless abandon. So, if you ever see a "Don't try this at home" warning, just know that somewhere out there, a water hose generation kid gave it a shot first.

I PARENT WITH SARCASM AND SNACKS.

I AM A MIX OF GRIT, GRACE, AND GRANDMA'S TUPPERWARE.

I AM TOO GROWN TO CARE ABOUT YOUR OPINION, BUT PETTY ENOUGH TO PUT IT IN THE GROUP CHAT.

I AM NOT BOSSY, I AM JUST AGGRESSIVELY RIGHT... ALL THE TIME.

I'M THE PLOT TWIST IN YOUR BORING-AZZ STORY.

I RELEASE WHAT NO LONGER SERVES ME, EXCEPT SARCASM—THAT SHIT STAYS FOREVER.

I KEEP MY THOUGHTS TO MYSELF BECAUSE HR IS TIRED OF HEARING ABOUT ME.

I MUTE, SMILE, AND MENTALLY FILE COWORKERS UNDER "NOT MY CIRCUS."

I LEARNED CONFIDENCE FROM THE PLAYGROUND, SARCASM FROM MY FRIENDS, AND PATIENCE FROM REWINDING VHS TAPES.

I SURVIVED TETHERBALL INJURIES, QUESTIONABLE CAFETERIA PIZZA, AND MY MOM'S "BECAUSE I SAID SO"—I CAN HANDLE ANYTHING.

PACIFIC BELL
STOP
50¢
PUBLIC PHONE
COLLECT CALLS
$5.50
DIAL 0
DIAL *11
MARQUE EL 0
MARQUE *11

BOUNDARIES & PEACE

I DESERVE LOVE, RESPECT, AND THE LAST DAMN SLICE.

Growing up, the last slice of pizza was basically a battlefield. You had to negotiate, distract, or just flat-out claim it before someone else got greedy. It wasn't just about the food; it was about standing your ground and knowing your worth, even if that meant a little playful sass.

We didn't grow up with participation trophies or safe spaces; we learned early that respect was earned, love was shown through actions, and if you wanted that last slice, you had to be ready to fight for it.

So, yeah, I deserve all of those things, and if you don't agree... well, I hope you like cold pizza.

I AM EMOTIONALLY AVAILABLE....UNLESS IT REQUIRES TALKING ABOUT FEELINGS BEFORE COFFEE.

I AM A BEACON OF CHILL...UNLESS SOMEONE PUTS THEIR CART IN THE MIDDLE OF THE AISLE.

I ATTRACT PEACE, NOT PEOPLE WHO TEXT "K" AND DISAPPEAR.

I HAVE THE PATIENCE OF A SAINT—OR AT LEAST SOMEONE WHO HIDES WINE IN A COFFEE CUP.

Back in the day, patience wasn't something you learned from apps or meditation; it came from waiting for your favorite song to play on the radio, sitting through dial-up noises just to get online, or standing in line for the latest VHS release.

Now, patience means sitting through endless "Are we there yet?" questions or surviving another Zoom meeting that could've been an email. Sometimes, that patience comes with a little extra help: a hidden sip tucked away like a secret from those carefree afternoons when time moved more slowly and the biggest worry was who got the last Tang packet.

Patience runs deep, but a little nostalgic trickery never hurts.

I APPRECIATE OPEN-DOOR POLICIES, ESPECIALLY WHEN I WALK RIGHT PAST THEM.

I TREASURE THE SIMPLE THINGS, LIKE HANDWRITTEN NOTES, PHOTO ALBUMS, AND SUMMER RAIN.

I'VE LEARNED THAT PROTECTING MY PEACE ISN'T SELFISH; IT'S SURVIVAL. I GUARD IT THE WAY I ONCE GUARDED MY MIXTAPES, BECAUSE

SOME THINGS ARE TOO PRECIOUS TO LET ANYONE FAST-FORWARD THROUGH.

I CHOOSE INNER HARMONY....BUT IF YOU DOUBLE-BOOK ME, YOU'RE CHOOSING VIOLENCE.

I FLOW WITH EASE... UNTIL SOMEONE SAYS, "LET'S CIRCLE BACK." THEN I FLOW RIGHT OUT THE DOOR.

I HONOR MY CALM...BUT IF YOU REPLY "PER MY LAST EMAIL," PREPARE FOR CHAOS.

SELF-LOVE & HUMOR

I TRUST MYSELF... BUT I ALSO CHECK IF I LOCKED THE DOOR FOUR TIMES.

It's like my brain's got two channels playing at once: one saying, "You got this, no problem," and the other whispering, "Wait...did you really lock it, or just think you did?"

I remember one time, I locked the door, started walking to my car, then halfway there, I had to turn right back around. Checked again. Walked off. Turned back. Maybe even a third time, just to be sure. It's not about doubting myself; it's more like life taught me the hard way that sometimes the universe just likes to mess with you.

Back in the day, we didn't have smart locks or alarms; you had to remember, and sometimes that memory game wouldn't cut you any slack. I trust myself to handle whatever life throws my way...but if you catch me sneaking back inside to check the lock again, don't call me crazy. I'm just seasoned, thorough, like a good Walkman rewinding the tape until it's just right.

TODAY, I CHOOSE GRACE....AND IF THAT FAILS, I CHOOSE CARBS.

I AM IN CONTROL OF MY EMOTIONS...80 PERCENT OF THE TIME. OKAY, 60 PERCENT...MAYBE 40 PERCENT.

I MOVE WITH PURPOSE...AND SOMETIMES, ADVIL.

I LOVE HARD, VIBE DEEP, AND NAP OFTEN.

I AM BALANCED...SLIGHTLY OFF-CENTER, BUT BALANCED.

I'm kind of like the old rabbit ears on the TV, one side bent a little more than the other, but if you held it just right (and maybe put a little foil on the end), the picture came through clear.

Life taught us early that perfect balance doesn't exist; you just shift your weight, roll with the punches, and keep your footing, even when the ground wobbles. We learned to handle the chaos of siblings hogging the phone line, parents telling us to be home "when the streetlights come on," and trying to record our favorite song off the radio without catching the DJ's voice.

I may be a little tilted at times, but I'm standing: steady enough to keep going, and just crooked enough to keep it interesting.

I AM PATIENT, EVEN WHEN A CHILD ASKS "WHY?" FOR THE THIRTY-SEVENTH TIME BEFORE 9:00 A.M.

I LOVE THE PERSON I'VE BECOME, BUT I'D STILL HIGH-FIVE MY YOUNGER SELF FOR GETTING ME HERE WITHOUT A HELMET.

I'VE LEARNED THAT LOVING MYSELF MEANS LAUGHING AT MY OWN STORIES, EVEN THE ONES THAT END WITH ME SAYING, "AND THAT'S HOW I ALMOST GOT GROUNDED FOR LIFE."

I CHOOSE PEACE... UNLESS SOMEONE EATS MY LEFTOVERS. THEN I CHOOSE VOLUME.

I RADIATE CONFIDENCE, EVEN IF MY READING GLASSES ARE CURRENTLY ON TOP OF MY HEAD.

I TRUST THE PROCESS....AS LONG AS IT DOESN'T INVOLVE DIAL-UP SPEED PATIENCE.

WATER HOSE VIBES

IF I CAN SURVIVE HOSE WATER AND SECONDHAND SMOKE IN A STATION WAGON, I CAN SURVIVE YOUR LITTLE "URGENT" GROUP TEXT.

I remember summers where the car smelled of old leather, Dad's cigarettes, and the faint tang of leftover snacks. We'd drink garden hose water, laughing as it splashed on our hands, while the sun baked the roof above us. Life was messy, loud, and imperfect, but it taught me patience, resilience, and how to find joy in the little things. So, yes, a frantic group text is nothing—I've been trained to weather storms far bigger than a ping.

I RADIATE COURAGE. I LICKED NINE-VOLT BATTERIES FOR FUN. YOUR "FEAR OF FAILURE" IS ADORABLE.

I PLAYED LAWN DARTS BAREFOOT. YOUR "RISK ASSESSMENT" CAN HAVE SEVERAL SEATS.

I CLIMBED TREES BAREFOOT. EVERY CHALLENGE IS JUST ANOTHER BRANCH.

I USED PAY PHONES THAT PROBABLY HAD EVERY GERM ALIVE. MY IMMUNE SYSTEM BOWS TO NO ONE.

I CHOOSE GROWTH. I CLIMBED EVERY TREE BAREFOOT, GOT SPLINTERS, AND CALLED IT CHILDHOOD.

I AM THE SURVIVOR OF METAL SLIDES, GRAVEL DRIVEWAYS, AND QUESTIONABLE CASSEROLES.

I AM THE SOUND OF A SCREEN DOOR SLAMMING AT DUSK— UNBOTHERED AND FREE.

I AM THE DEFINITION OF FORTITUDE. MY FIRST ENERGY DRINK WAS HOSE WATER.

My first energy drink wasn't Red Bull or Monster; it was hose water that tasted like hot pennies straight from the sun. And let me tell you, we lined up for it like it was holy water. No electrolytes, no BPA-free bottles, just liquid copper running through our veins. You didn't sip it cute, either; you cranked that hose, waited for the boiling hot blast to pass, and took your chances. That's why the water hose generation doesn't flinch at chaos. We were raised on hydration that doubled as a tetanus shot.

I AM THE WATER HOSE GENERATION: THE GENERATION THAT RAISED ITSELF, DRANK FROM THE WATER HOSE, AND STILL MANAGED TO LOOK THIS DAMN GOOD. NAMA-STAY OUT OF MY FACE.

1000
POLAROID LAND CAMERA

JOURNALING PROMPTS

Blockbuster Nights

Think back to wandering the aisles of Blockbuster, debating VHS vs. DVD, hoping your movie wasn't already rented out. How are your decision-making skills and disappointment now compared to then?

Mixtape Messages

Every mixtape told a story, whether it was for a crush, a friend, or yourself. Write about one collection of songs that captured the hopes of your younger self. What is different about how you express your feelings and creativity now?

Pay Phone Courage

Dropping coins into a pay phone to call someone often required guts. Reflect on a time when you took a bold step in your youth. How does that same courage show up in your adult choices?

Streetlight Rules

We knew it was time to go home when the streetlights flickered on. Write about the unspoken rules or boundaries that shaped your childhood. How do you set limits for yourself or others today?

Atari to AI

From Pong to PlayStation to smartphones, we've lived through every technological shift. What has your journey with technology taught you about resilience, flexibility, and adaptability?

PASSING NOTES

Before texting, we folded notes into secret shapes and passed them in class. Write about one note you wish you could send back to your younger self. What reply would you want your future self to give you?

Saturday Morning Cartoons

Saturday mornings meant cereal, pajamas, and cartoons. Which shows sparked your imagination or shaped your humor? How do you keep that sense of wonder alive now?

Roller Rink Reflections

Skating in circles to the same songs was freedom and fun. Write about a cycle you've broken in your life, and one joyful cycle you've chosen to keep spinning.

Dial-Up Patience

Waiting for the internet to connect taught us patience (or tested it). How do you handle "buffering" moments in your life now? Where has patience become one of your greatest strengths?

Lunch Box Legacy

From PB&Js to Dunkaroos, our lunch boxes told stories. What simple pleasures or comforts from your past still show up in your daily life?

Road Trip Soundtracks

Whether it was a mixtape in the car or the radio on full blast, every trip had its soundtrack. Write about the songs that shaped your youth and the songs that describe your life now.

Trapper Keeper Dreams

Those bold, bright binders kept our world organized (sort of). What tools, rituals, or mindsets help you keep order and balance in your life today?

Pencil-and-Cassette Rewinds

We used pencils to rewind tangled tapes. Write about a time in your life that felt "tangled." How did you find a way to rewind, repair, and keep moving forward?

WATER HOSE HYDRATION

We drank from the hose without a second thought. Write about a fearless moment from your youth. Where could you use a little more of that fearless spirit today?

Polaroid Moments

Polaroids weren't perfect, but they captured something real. What's one imperfect memory that turned out to be more beautiful than perfection ever could have been?

RECESS RESETS

Recess gave us permission to play, run, and let go. What does "recess" look like in your adult life? How do you give yourself permission to pause and play?

Library Card Freedom

A library card was the ultimate passport to new worlds. What forms of learning, reading, or curiosity still spark joy and growth in you today?

Analog Friendships

We maintained friendships without texts or social media. Write about a friendship that has stood the test of time. What makes it different from the way connections are built today?

Backyard Adventures

From hide-and-seek to building forts, the backyard was a kingdom. What is a childhood adventure that shaped your imagination? How do you still nurture that adventurous spirit?

Water Hose Generation Gratitude Playlist

Think of five things from your water hose generation youth that built your resilience. Now, list five things you're grateful for today that keep you grounded.

First Concert Energy

Think back to your very first concert: the music, the clothes, the crowd. How did that experience shape the way you express yourself or find community now?

Mall Rat Adventures

The mall was more than shopping; it was social life. Reflect on what those days taught you about independence, friendships, or fitting in. Where do you find that same sense of belonging now?

Board Game Rivalries

From Monopoly meltdowns to Uno wars, games tested patience and strategy. Write about what you learned from childhood play and how it shows up in the way you handle competition today.

Handwritten Memories

Whether it was yearbook notes, pen pals, or doodles in the margins, handwriting captured our stories. Write about one written memory that still lingers and how you preserve memories today.

CUE/REVIEW & AUTO STOP MECHANISM
PHONES
MIC
VOLUME
LEVEL INDICATOR

CONCLUSION

If you've made it to the end of this book, congratulations—not because it was hard to read, but because in between these pages, you remembered pieces of yourself you might've forgotten. The kid who could entertain themselves for hours with a jump rope. The teenager who knew every lyric to every song on a mixtape. The grown-up who still carries a little bit of that freedom, grit, and stubborn joy in their back pocket.

We are not just a generation; we're a vibe. We've been the bridge between "Call me back after 9:00 p.m. when it's free" and "Why haven't they texted me back yet?" We've learned to pivot, to adapt, and to laugh, even when life hands us a plot twist no one warned us about. And we've done it without losing that spark that made us who we are.

So, here's your final affirmation: You are still that kid who came home with grass stains and stories to tell. You are still resourceful, still resilient, and still ridiculously capable, even if you now need readers to see the menu. The world may have changed, but your ability to thrive, adapt, and throw in a sarcastic one-liner hasn't gone anywhere.

Now go out there, live loud, and keep those water hose vibes alive...because the streetlights aren't on yet, and we're just getting started.

Connect with me online for more laughs, side-eye, and straight-up Gen X wisdom on TikTok, Instagram, YouTube, and Facebook (@SmartAzzAuntie).

—Smart Azz Auntie

ABOUT THE AUTHOR

Rhonda James, best known online as **Smart Azz Auntie**, is the unapologetic voice of Gen X realness with a side of sarcasm and soul. A former corporate trainer turned content creator, Rhonda serves up equal parts wit and wisdom, channeling the lived experience of the water hose generation into content that's as hilarious as it is healing. Through her viral videos and sharp-tongued affirmations, she reminds grown folks that it's okay to be tired, petty, and powerful, all at the same time. Based in the Raleigh, North Carolina area, Rhonda continues to create content that speaks to the latchkey kids, the mixtape makers, and the emotionally exhausted champions of common sense. *Smartass Affirmations: Wisdom from the Water Hose Generation* is her love letter to them all.

Mango Publishing, established in 2014, publishes an eclectic list of books by diverse authors—both new and established voices—on topics ranging from business, personal growth, women's empowerment, LGBTQ studies, health, and spirituality to history, popular culture, time management, decluttering, lifestyle, mental wellness, aging, and sustainable living. We were named 2019 and 2020's #1 fastest growing independent publisher by Publishers Weekly. Our success is driven by our main goal, which is to publish high-quality books that will entertain readers as well as make a positive difference in their lives.

Our readers are our most important resource; we value your input, suggestions, and ideas. We'd love to hear from you—after all, we are publishing books for you!

Please stay in touch with us and follow us at:

Facebook: Mango Publishing
Twitter: @MangoPublishing
Instagram: @MangoPublishing
LinkedIn: Mango Publishing
Pinterest: Mango Publishing
Newsletter: mangopublishinggroup.com/newsletter

Join us on Mango's journey to reinvent publishing, one book at a time.

www.ingramcontent.com/pod-product-compliance
Lightning Source LLC
Jackson TN
JSHW031848251025
92584JS00001B/1

* 9 7 8 1 6 8 4 8 1 8 9 4 5 *